Poems
from
the
Rocky
Mountains

A. Albert Aguero

WestBow®
PRESS
A DIVISION OF THOMAS NELSON
& ZONDERVAN

WestBow Press books may be ordered through booksellers or by contacting:

WestBow Press
A Division of Thomas Nelson & Zondervan
1663 Liberty Drive
Bloomington, IN 47403
www.westbowpress.com
1 (866) 928-1240

ISBN: 978-1-4908-5200-3 (sc)
ISBN: 978-1-4908-5201-0 (e)

Library of Congress Control Number: 2014916370

Printed in the United States of America.

WestBow Press rev. date: 11/07/2014

Dedication

This book is dedicated, with lots of love, to the memory of my wonderful wife, Carol Aguero, an excellent mother, grandmother, and great-grandmother, who also loved oil painting and poetry, as seen in the illustration of the front cover of this book, and in the poem "The Heart Knows," in the Appendix, respectively, and who also enjoyed reading fiction, and enjoyed music.

A. Albert Aguero

Acknowledgements

It is a real pleasure to thank anyone who may have contributed with the process of making Poems From the Rocky Mountains a reality, which includes you, the reader, and those behind the scene who used the technical skills and professional knowledge to make this book useful to grade school, high school, college students, parents and the general public.

Carol Chalk Aguero did an excellent job of achieving content closure with her poem, "The Heart knows." Thanks Carol, for contributing that unusually beautiful poem to this poetic collection. But also, thanks for your permission to use a photo of your original oil painting of the Boulder Flatirons on the front cover of the book.

A million thanks to Lee Aguero for his suggestions and literary support and advice about the artistic quality of this book project. Also, without the computer technological assistance from Lee, the realization of this project would have been impossible.

Clifford Scott Aguero's poem, "Grey Leaves," as part of the process is indispensable to the book content closure and a wonderful example of how to express feelings at any reality level. Thanks again Clifford, for volunteering also your computer expertise to this project.

Most sincere thanks to Johnathan David Aguero, a professional Denver photographer, who has enhanced the quality of this book with a photo of Carol Chalk Aguero's oil painting for the front cover, a photo which Johnathan took in the San Juan Mountains for the back cover and the author's photo for the inside of the back cover.

A most sincere "Thank you both" to Austin Eblen and Barbra Carter, publishing consultant and check-in coordinator at WestBow Press, respectively, for their kind and expert assistance in the process of completing this book project.

It makes it very difficult to express the deep gratitude that Betsy Stroomer, Director of the Lafayette, Colorado Public Library deserves for her invaluable help in the different library science expertise areas relevant to this book project. Thanks again to Betsy and to the City of Lafayette for hiring her.

About the Author

In the middle of World War II, A. Albert Aguero volunteered to take military training with one of the United States military service branches in Heredia, Costa Rica. His goal was to be of service to the United States if, and as needed, in the on-going war. At the time of his military training, he was a junior in high school.

By the generosity, thoughtfulness, courtesy and efforts of the National Congress of Costa Rica, the State Department of the United States, the American Embassy in San José, Costa Rica and the Institute of International Education, A. Albert Aguero was awarded grants to study in the United States.

The author attended the following institutions of higher education: the University of Costa Rica, Wellesley University, University of Denver, Dallas Theological Seminary, Texas Christian University, the University of Texas at Arlington, Texas, the University of Colorado, Boulder Campus and Covington Theological Seminary in Georgia.

A. Albert Aguero was awarded an Associate's Degree in Education, a Bachelor's Degree in Educational Psychology, a Master's Degree in Clinical Psychology, an additional Master's Degree in Counseling Psychology and a Doctor of Philosophy Degree (Ph.D.), Magna Cum Laude, in Christian Counseling.

A linguist and psychologist, A. Albert Aguero retired from the Boulder, Colorado, School District and upon retirement, he founded Lafayette Alcohol Education and Therapy, an outpatient clinic for the diagnosis and treatment of alcohol/illegal drug use/abuse and related mental health issues requiring individual therapy, group facilitation and marriage, couple and family counseling, including all aspects of alcohol/drug use/abuse. He was clinical director, as well as owner of Lafayette Alcohol Education and Therapy for the last 32 years of his professional career.

While teaching at the Boulder School District, A. Albert Aguero was on leave of absence from the school district for one year to be the Director of the Junior-Year-Abroad Program at the University of Costa Rica for the University of Kansas at Lawrence, Kansas and for the University of Colorado, Boulder Campus. He and his family traveled by car from Boulder to San José, Costa Rica. That year, as a good-will ambassador, he taught graduate psychology courses at the University of Costa Rica.

In the field of poetry, A. Albert Aguero has received several editor's awards and his poems have been featured in the best-poems-and-poets-of-the-year-anthologies of poetry. com many times. Further recognition and awards for his poetry include the Outstanding-Achievement-in-Poetry Silver Bowl, the International-Poet-of-Merit Silver Bowl, the Poetry Laureate Certificate, International Society of Poets Distinguished Member and induction into the International Poetry Hall of Fame in 1996.

Preface

The sources of this book date back to my childhood days in San Ramón, Province of Alajuela, Costa Rica. Down there, whenever we visited friends or relatives in the mountains, after supper, we gathered in their family room to recite poetry. In preparation for any unexpected trip to visit significant ones in the countryside, I memorized a poem by a local poet, Lisímaco Chavarría. The poem expressed feelings of anxiety about dying and also, about things which the poet hoped that the community people could do in order to make his funeral pleasant, and to have a peaceful resting place for his human remains. He was dying from tuberculosis, incurable at that time.

Feelings like in above case may be part of the process of dying and of being born also, because as soon as the new-born baby takes in her/his first self-breath, the baby starts reacting to his/her environment. At this point, it is possible to observe the intensity level of his/her post-natal emotions which express the baby's feelings through sound and body language.

The following additional examples of feelings as an indispensable component of poetry writing will help the reader to understand how I arrived at the conclusion that I should write this book of poetry. In the Jewish culture, as we notice in the Old Testament, we have the poetic books of The Bible, prevailingly, Psalms, Job and Proverbs and they all put emphasis on feelings and behavior(s) which take place under different conditions, times and places. The main theme in those books, as well as in any other poetic writings in the culture is pleading for guidance from Jehovah, as well as praise for His faithfulness.

Pedro Calderón de la Barca of the Spanish-literary-Golden-Age period wrote the play "Life is a Dream," in verse, to tell the Spanish society that life is an illusion, a dream, that everybody dreams what he/she is though no one may understand it. Segismundo, the main protagonist of this dream, dreams that he is trapped in his self-prison and dreaming of hope for positive changes in life.

Poet Neftalí Ricardo Reyes Basoalto, pen name Pablo Neruda, from Chile and a recipient of the 1971 Nobel Prize for literature, uses poetry writing to release his feelings of anger against society and the political system of his country for the injustices in dealing with the underprivileged class of the Chilean population.

English Poet Laureate Alfred Lord Tennyson uses his prestigious literary and social position to release feelings of hopefulness which finds its climax in the poem "Crossing the Bar." After going over the threshold between physical life and eternity, the poet hopes to see his Guide, his Pilot in a one-on-one encounter: feelings of hope for eternal peace and no sadness upon his departure for those left behind.

Robert Frost uses poetry to express his feelings about nature as well as about social and human behavior in general: decision making and effective communication to prevent any level of disruption in relationships. We can find this style of poetry in his poem "Mending Wall."

The reasons to write this book of poetry are implied in my cultural background, training and experience. As a linguist and psychologist, I have dedicated all my life to helping anyone in need of my services as a psychotherapist. Reading and/or writing poetry is therapeutic and it is something which you can do on your own. And this is the message which I am trying to convey to anyone reading this book. And this message is validated by the fact that poetry can be defined as the art of expressing the needs of the "self" in order to cope with feelings, problems and stress, wherever those feelings may be found: the conscious, subconscious and/or unconscious. Then, and only then, can we start searching for the connection between individual feelings and national and international events. Hopefully, above reasons will enhance the reader's awareness of the benefit of using poetry as self-therapy: mental-health-quality improvement and increased enjoyment of life.

Introduction

It would be a real pleasure to present these poems to you, the reader of this book, in person, so that I might tell you what to expect from its contents. However, I can tell you that beyond this introductory statement, I sincerely hope that you may find in this book, as many poems as possible which may relate to infinite experiences in your present and past and which, in the not-so-distant future, you may use to cheer yourself up and to enhance the sunny side of life and add to your positive life quality.

You may want to start with our six-year-old, A. J., who took about 30 minutes of his time to introduce himself to me, and talk about one of his fishing adventures. His parents were yelling at him and telling him to get out of their office, go out of the building, in the street, and find something with which to play. I was waiting for the next therapy session to start and my door to the hallway was open a crack. Through the crack space, I saw one of his eyes peeking into my office. I walked to the door, opened it, introduced myself and invited A. J. to come into my office. I asked him what was his most important activity with his friends and he mentioned fishing and went on to tell me about his fishing trip to the Wyoming/Colorado State border, where he hooked a humongous shark, in the middle of winter in a river pond, while his cousin was catching only tiny minnows.

Another poem could be the one about Corla's wingless flying adventure, up in the sky in a moonlight night in Corla's husband's "Moonlight Dream," or the poem about the grade-school boy, daydreaming in the classroom of going over the horizon on the neighbor's mare, which you may find in "Childhood Reality." But if you just want to relax at home after work, just take off your shoes, lie down in your couch or sit in a comfortable chair in your garden or by the swimming pool and share a poem with your child or any relative or friend. I know that you will find in this book something to enhance the joy of living in a pleasant and creative way.

Contents

Universality of Poetry

In the turbulence of the Amazon-Orinoco confluence,
For miles and miles and then, forever apart;
In the exuberance of joy and sadness of the ghetto dives
In Denver, Río, San José or the peace of a rainbow
At sundown over a marshland,
Or the Ute Indians in a powwow
Chanting while doing the Bear Dance,
Everywhere in nature: land, water or sky
Poetry is dormant but very much alive
In the legacy of kingdoms
And the political right to be what they are;
In the charisma buildings cream–top–living style,
Filled with spiritual poverty and occasional lies
And bubbling with fear notes and joylessness;
Feelings everywhere are ready to be awakened by poets
From the depth of their sources
To the openness of the human mind,
And propelled into the process of becoming,
To show you and me that life is life,
And that it is nothing that anyone may capture
To be kept from eternally growing
In the physical and spiritual realm: poetry,
Always ready to become alive.

The American Symphony

Nothing can overpower the euphoric feeling
Of belonging to a great nation,
Which we are proud to proclaim,
With all its faults and shining deeds
In tiny towns and large metropolis,
Through prosperous and also inhospitable years.
We are supportive and abstain from judging
Negative forces affecting our welfare,
Defending what others criticize with disdain,
For this is a land of free thinking,
And mistakes of any consequential impact,
Our nation can always delete.
From the Canadian to the Mexican border:
Lakes, rivers, Appalachian and Rocky Mountains,
Valleys and plains from California to New York,
And the thunderous Mississippi in-between,
The hustle and bustle of industrial momentum,
The angelic singing of Negro spirituals in Harlem
Or the melodious blues and jazz tempo of the south,
Fine arts, technological advance, all we have.
And when the music, religious beliefs and sports,
When the symphony of everything American sounds,
I thank God for whatever part
You and I, in this orchestration may have.

A. J.'s Shark

Somewhere in a forest
Where blue birds live
And house finches build their nests,
Under a ten-foot waterfall,
A. J. went fishing one day:
A short pole, small hook, a huge worm,
And guess what!
He caught a humongous shark!
Telling about the adventure,
He pictures himself under the fall,
Surrounded by pines, snow and all
Line wrapped around the tree trunk,
The beast swimming in circles really fast,
And A. J. holding on to the line.
The furious shark, 'round and 'round,
Peeling off the tree's bark.
A. J.'s arms can't stretch enough
To show the shark's size
And tell me how exciting
The fishing adventure was.

Emily

A granddaughter who always smiles a lot,
And always cares about co-workers, classmates,
And all her relatives and friends,
Who always share her love.

We all enjoy her poems and paintings,
Since she was seven or before,
Portraying nature's beauty to share
With dad, grandma, grandpa,
And some others she can trust.
Beautiful and healthy as a fresh breath,
Of early-morning-Rocky-Mountain air.

An excellent worker and student,
Guiding tours at the State Capitol Building
To fulfill requirements for her degree,
And very appreciative of the opportunities
That she may receive.

Maybe we overlook things
Not so perfect about Emily
Because she is so unusual,
And almost impossible
To find anyone, anywhere, like her.

Autumn Morning Scene

Autumn leaves
Floating down the stream . . .,
Some are red, some are yellow,
None of color green.
Others above the water,
Twirling as they wish,
Carelessly playing like children
Skipping along with the wind,
Between the water and the trees.
The morning sun
That in the summer peeks
Through the thickness
Of the leaves,
Now watches among the branches
And the leafless twigs,
While the trout prance and waltz,
Hoping to catch a morning meal
Above the water,
Under the trees.

Freedom Pursuit Modeling
at the Olympics

She became a freedom forerunner
In the Down-Under Land,
Bearing two flags:
One in her heart,
The other,
In her right hand.
The universal and thunderous crowd,
Cheered her on to the finish line
Of a well-deserved-olympic crown:
One long stride at a time,
The champion's heart pounding very fast,
As her vision captures the ideal reward
Inspired by her genetic make-up:
Not to seek the gold that glitters
But the triumph for her people to regard.

The heroine showed the world
That success is for anyone,
Who tries her or his best,
Regardless of nationality,
Religious creed or race.

Dignity, Freedom and Poetry

The source of dignity is freedom
And the source of poetry is life,
And dignity and life
Cannot be taken apart.

That is why, like the spring water
On the sloping mountainside,
Poetry cannot be stopped,
Or dammed, neither can it hide.

It bursts up and out of the "self,"
But it is forced out by inspiration,
For its components are motivation
And feelings to sustain interest
And to stay alive.

Poetry can soar way, way up,
So high that no one can capture it;
No one can possess it
And it is anchored to freedom
In its search for universal light;
No one can stop it or force down,
And if anyone tries to break
Its connection to life,
It would break away and go on
Beyond the human horizon,
Not to hide but to stay free and survive.

Your Fare Will Be Fair

Life is a boat sailing through a storm,
Rocked by waves,
Lighted by sunshine rays;
At times terrifying,
At times unstable
And no one can say
When its calm will arrive,
Or how long will remain.

If in serenity it approaches your port
And you might be there,
Waiting for ways to sail along,
Just be prepared
To accept whatever self-reward
You may have to use
To pay for your fare.

From Feelings to Art

Tears sleeping within your eyes.
A feelings nest so tight
That makes them cry.
You don't have to understand
What those feelings are about.
They have a nest,
And that's what makes them count.
Some left your heart
In search of solace
And when ready to depart,
They found the gates unopened
And themselves unable to return
To where they came from . . .,
But through the ink flow
Of your ballpoint,
They turned into human art.

A Stream of Gems

A stream of gems flowing from my heart:
Emeralds for my hopes,
Rubies for times past,
Diamonds for the tears that have dried up
Within my loved one's eyes,
Feelings I wish that I could trap
In a net within my heart
But fast slipping into my mind.
And I feel a cry that I cannot contain,
Neither can I let it out,
Tearing my soul apart.
It is a heavy load
Which I cannot recognize:
Bittersweet, were I to ask
Anyone my feelings to compart,
A stream of gems that gushes out
From the bottom of my heart
But stops upon arriving to my mind . . .,
A stream of gems
That has never been mined.

Fool's Gold Migration to the North

They come across
The Río Grande,
Searching for the golden trees,
Which drop the leaves,
That turn to fading green
Upon falling on the ground
And no one, but no one,
Neither they can perceive.
Wet or dry,
They almost always
Make it to the opposite side,
Across the Río Grande
And walk a straight line,
Through deserts,
Mountains and human kind,
To the magical destination
Where there is always,
An unsuspected legal ban.

Poverty Behind

He has a pair of pants
With two holes:
One in front and one behind,
And he knows
That the things
Which one values most,
Seldom last long enough.
It is kind of handy though,
To have this pair of pants,
Because when it's really hot,
And he doesn't have
Air conditioning or a half-way-
Decent fan, if it's windy,
He can open a window
In line with a door facing out,
Stand in the line
To enjoy the breeze,
Going right through his pants.

U.S.A. Soldier's Hope

Not promises of brilliant things to come
Where none ever existed before,
But comfort for physical pain and distress,
For feelings of loneliness and sadness for all
That at Christmas time invade self-images and love;
Laughter produced by human compassion
For soldiers obeying the service call
To keep the good name of our nation afloat,
To support family and friends left behind at home,
Knowing that the Susans, Peters and Seans
For a long time have been gone.
But this Christmas, thank God,
Many soldiers will have some hours of fun
At the battlefront watching a show:
Singing, dancing and hilarious jokes,
Giving our service women and men
A well-deserved break and hope,
Hope, with capital H, of course,
By our kindest, greatest comedian:
Who else but our beloved Bob Hope.

The Last Trip Home

The way home, whichever it is,
Is not now
What years back is to be.
After flying all day,
He opened the front door
And when she walked down the hallway,
He dashed to meet her,
Captured her big smile and said,
"Mother, it is great to see you again."
For she was getting old;
Her age showing in her gray hair.
And after just a few days
Of visiting with her,
Before leaving for the airport
To board the jet to return home,
She looked at him with a sad smile
In her wrinkled face and said,
"I hope to see you real soon,
Before departing for my heavenly
Dwelling place."

Tropical Rain Memories

He hears the tap . . ., tap . . ., tap . . .,
Of the tropical rain,
Way down south . . .,
Further than the Rio Grande.
He can hear it, deep in his mind,
From way back
In his native land,
Back where he was born . . .,
When he was there.
And the tap . . ., tap . . ., tap . . .,
Fading away
Through dancing droplets
On the ground,
He will always hear,
Until he arrives at the place,
Where for evermore,
He will abide.

At a Country Cottage Breakfast

Everything rolls on the western plains:
The cattle and the round bales of hay.
Before my eyes, the machinery;
The Rocky Mountains, in my brain.

"We've been down this road before,"
Said the waitress to the cowboy."
She's talking neighborly, he's trying love:
Week-end love away from the ranch,
Overnight ardor,
Nothing less, nothing more.
And the lady may have served,
In more than one way, his kind before.
But on the western plains,
Everything goes on and on
And the cowboy knowing so,
Tries his rolling behavior,
Before breakfast time once more,
While the tumbleweeds,
Round bales of hay and human hormones,
Western style, keep rolling along.

Not in Line

The sun peeking over the mountain top;
Tombstones everywhere, guarding bones
And six bodies under a heavy metal box,
Keeping pace with a somber tone.

A long line from the wake site,
On the path of love to the chapel,
Where mourners wait forlorn.
An unwanted visitor
Keeping some distance from the procession
With tears and sobs,
For he is not welcome anymore,
And the line, snaking around the trees,
And the prodigal son,
Sneaking behind the shrubs
With tunnel-vision steps,
Directed to where the bell's toll,
Summons the outsider to go.

And suddenly,
Looking down into the final resting box,
There shows a voice flashback
Whispering:
"Welcome son, I love you so."

Dream Bridge

The hollow of life where we dream what we are,
With a bridge between sides
And turmoil below the bridge underside.
You walk halfway to the end to find out
Whether you are playing your part right,
To share success with friends and enemies alike,
And go the last half to get to the dawning light,
Just past the inconsistencies of life,
And you arrive at the threshold
Between the bridge and the solid-dream road
Where you stepped in a void,
From where you could sense the turbulence,
And look down on the chasm above the water below
But on the downfall, you grabbed a side,
Thus disrupting a terminal blow;
One foot on one side, hands on the other
To push yourself up to safe ground,
And go back to try the way
Around the crack of life
To go beyond the bridge,
Beyond adversity where we dream what we are
From within our chaos and risk only
The fantasy on the dream bridge,
Above the river of life.

Christmas-Time Masks

Ambulating masks wherever you go.
Some show signs of dejection
From years before: untouchable torture
That makes you sad,
Printed smiles of indifference
About everything in life.
Some may look meek,
Meekness not very deep,
For when you bruise their ego
They may attack
With feelings so tense . . .,
Like the claw of an eagle
Ready to snatch the prey
While still in flight.

All life is focused
On the peace of Christmas time,
At the end of which,
Some masks may disappear,
Others may start to relax.

Summer Departure

An air of quietness pushing along
Bundles and bundles of sunshine gold.
The trees and the breeze
Will not interfere at all,
For autumn is waiting
For rain and the snow to fall.
The fish in the streams
Are getting ready
To seek shelter in warmer places
Where freezing weather
May not be merciless . . .,
Perhaps in the pools of the meadow.
The birds fly south
And the whales circle the world around.
The folks are bringing out
The snow boots and warmer wear,
For the air of quietness
Keeps pushing along,
Bundles and bundles of sunshine gold.

Human Lightness

Bodies walking in the dark;
Light never before internalized,
Eyes seeing but not perceiving
Anything from the mental outer field
Usually used to hide darkness:
Poverty in the heart,
Emptiness which sets the good traits apart
To ambulate away
When nothing appears refined,
Like silver or gold
That took the form of art,
Because the bodies,
Misguided by fear of the dark,
Froze in the obliviousness of the atmosphere,
Unable to capture the wisdom
Of human lightness.

Villanelle of Misunderstood Rustic Ways

Those who live in the mountain land
Have always seen life's happy side
And city folks their ways don't understand,

Not even with piles and piles of castle sand
And never close to the city could abide,
Those who live in the mountain land.

Many times they are socially bland
And many times, socially collide
And city folks their ways don't understand.

They may play with the village band,
Or labor and celebrate side by side,
Those who live in the mountain land.

They are never depending on a magic wand,
Their social life is narrow, not so wide
And city folks their ways don't understand.

In frigid places, their food is canned,
For night light they use lanterns with carbide,
Those who live in the mountain land,
And city folks their ways don't understand.

The Beauty of Essence

Tiny microscopic cells,
In tiny storage tubes within the brains,
In a vacuum
No one can relate to, or explain;
Microscopic cells floating
Up to an opening, searching for fresh air,
But, oh! They sense the beauty of nature,
And exposed to the Rocky Mountain air,
In contact with the atmosphere,
The cells turn into gorgeous, colorful butterflies,
And fairy-tale-like dragonflies;
But the beauty of nature
Entices them to avoid returning to the original shelter,
To stay out, enjoying beauty and freedom forever,
And not to vanish into thin air,
But be transformed into flora and fauna,
That every human eye may capture
To store in their brains,
Not realizing that essence never changes:
It always remains the same.

Psycho-Social Fusion

I dreamed that you and I,
Whoever you are,
Were going up, and up, and up,
Into the thickness of the sky
And there was a trail of light,
Trailing right behind us,
Following our newly-created path,
Squeezing through the heavy clouds,
But also gathering sunshine rays
From all around us
In every cloudy crack,
Unperceived by every rainbow in sight;
And you and I were becoming "we,"
United by the tightness of the clouds
But unaware of our mutual influence.
We never realized
That before we were "I's"
And now had become a "wesome two,"
Forging a new path for our lives.

Journey to Success

The life of joyful work in his childhood
As a daily newspaper boy,
Or running errands in the neighborhood,
Compensated now by intellectual joy,
Lingering in his adolescent mind,
With tape-style repetition as the train rides north,
Of memories past that were always kind,
Of memories that with the present will go forth.

The human ocean at Grand Central Station:
Stepping down and making his way
Through the masses-tunnel vision
Doesn't see or hear what others have to say.

Boarding the car on the night-railroad line
That will carry him to his final destination,
To accomplish what he always had in mind:
The ideal of achieving intellectual consummation.

The efforts in life's mental train are exhausting,
Dangerous like the edge of a sharp knife.
Is there any justice in blocking
What he always aspired in his life?

Her Friend Cottontail

She has a friend
On her way to work,
As she turns north
At the first-four-way stop.
Her friend's name is CTR,
For short,
And CTR comes out
From under a wooden fence,
To greet her as she walks by;
At times, CTR twitches his nose
And wiggles his ears,
And his rear-white-round flag
Goes up, to let his friend know
That everything is fine
But that he changed his mind,
And wants to lead
And hop . . ., hop . . ., hop . . .,
To get himself about six feet in front:
Frequent stops
Until CTR gets close,
And then, he hops to the side
Where he sees a rotten
Fence board, goes under
And through a pine-knot hole
Watches her go to the corner
To catch the next bus.

Raccoon Family Night Out

A hush . . ., hush . . ., hush inside the house,
From the rain,
Imposing its mellowness to insiders;
And past the walls, outside the windows,
The water slides down the silvery bark
Of a very old and huge cherry tree
With a branch at roof-top level,
Showing a spot where the raccoons
Stop momentarily to dig their claws,
To jump to the roof, with friends
From the neighborhood for family parties,
After hunting birds and squirrels,
All night long.

The water saturates the ground
Around the tree, turning its surroundings
Into a dark-looking sponge,
With night crawlers peeking out
From every tiny hole
And slithering out as fast as they can,
To keep from drowning
In the flooded ground.
And the hush . . ., from inner feelings
In the house rooms fades out gradually
As the rain departs
And the noisy raccoons in the chimney
Lie down to sleep through the day,
To get up next night
To have a family fun social again.

Routes to Life's Goals

Two routes leading to the same destination:
One narrow, in a gorge,
Between sky-hungry mountaintops;
The other, open space at a plateau,
Straight, no anxiety to travel on.
The one below, beautiful,
Under an emerald-green canopy,
Modest, hard-dusty path
With feelings mixed
In somber lack of love
Not filtering through the foliage above.
The high passage, free of love,
Indifferent to the human soul,
Taking longer to cross
The intervening space,
With many more years,
And time to imprint feelings and thoughts
To use as a guide and give life
Opportunities for compassion,
Honesty, assertiveness,
And think about the route below,
As something for others to choose,
Which is their right to do so.

Sonnet to Immigrants

. . . And made the blacks, the reds, the browns, the whites,
Created all to be in earth alike:
To play, to walk, to sail, to ride on bikes,
To ride on donkeys, feeling free and light,
To live the way the culture thinks is right
And look the way you want, perhaps a tyke.
But also use the right to work, to strike,
To keep the present goals and plans in sight

And migrants have to always rules respect:
The need to work, to be alert and strive,
To use the language even with defects,
To try the best in life to stay alive,
And rights are nothing bought, to steel, select;
To be open, nothing ever contrived.

Moonlight Dream

Up in the sky,
Patches of blue under the moon,
Sometimes dark,
What a surprise!
It looked like Corla riding a broom,
Playing a game, diving straight down
And bouncing up again.
The wind apparently combing her hair,
Her dress, if existed, skin tight.
But who cares what she looks like
Under the beautiful blue light.
Far into space, her silhouette
Enjoying her self-chase
In a playful pirouette.

Walking in her bedroom,
Hubby discovers that she was in bed,
And his dreaming mind had put Corla
Out in the bright shining space,
Chasing her silhouette.

The River of Life

The stream struggles from source to death
And conquers heights to find the way,
Snaking around boulders, dead or live trees
Competes for things it may need.
On the plains relaxed, in the mountains alert.
The breeze and the sunshine rays
Claims to own in the calm of the day
And when jumping, it sings with joy
Skipping around rocks, murmuring along
But through evil and good, never complains,
It has goals to attain.
Even while fighting debris
One may float down the current,
Learn to survive, bob up or go under,
Never again to revive,
While the fountain of life flows forever
Challenging nature's changing roles.

A Social Senior

You were a senior in high school,
Perhaps a senior in a college class,
And to you, it was a transitional design,
Never counting the years behind,
Neither those to come,
Maybe full of lust or love.
Later on, soul and body merchants introspect
At the whiteness on your head,
And the wrinkles on your face:
Sink-and-sewage-systems engineers,
Barbers, politicians, bankers,
Insurance agents, scam vultures,
Legal-system vendors,
All hands out:
The whole society in line;
And you are a senior, on social security,
Taken not as an achiever,
But something from the past.

At a Rehabilitation Clinic

Countless wheel chairs
In a straight line,
Slowly turning as they mark time,
Silently warning
Those in sight,
That life is headed
Aimlessly down to the ground:
Bodies bent forward
Sometimes with empty minds;
All instinctively following
The same line,
Like marbles aimed
At the same chuckhole:
Poor, wealthy, bright or dull
Proud and humble
Educated or not,
Their lives are rolling
Along with the chairs
And now, life's remaining reward
Depends upon how much love
Is given to them,
And how well they adjust
To what they get
In their daily life.

Echoes of Rain

A thunderous zigzag,
Rumbling and lightning
Between the trees
And around the houses,
Like the beating of drums
From snare to bass.
The descending rain
Plays melodious scales;
Not from musicians
Because the notes are enmeshed
In incomprehensible tones
Which need to be unraveled
By individual feelings and thoughts.
The variable-size drops
Fall on the leaves, the grass,
The flowers and rooftops
And gather in the gutter,
To slide down together
To their final destination
And to come back
As a spring reflection.

Lost Melodies

The twisting waters,
Of a childhood dream,
Running away from the pasture
In the meadow's green.
They came up against the mountains
But could not go uphill,
Then turned around
And went down past the rocks
Where they could sing songs,
Whispering songs,
As they went along;
But other sources they joined,
Not knowing
That they were to belong
To other twisting waters
Of a bigger stream below,
Where the peace of the meadow
And the whispering songs
Could not be heard sung
In the green of the meadow anymore.

Mississippi River Hypnotic Power

It was brown and roaring
Like a mate-searching lioness;
I was up on deck,
Mesmerized by the rolling waters
Crashing against barges
And anything else in the way.
The calliope was playing
Old southern tunes,
And the passengers were awaiting
The expected appearance
Of a full moon,
Peeking above the horizon
And pushing itself up
Over nature's enigmatic bar,
Simultaneously looking into my eyes
With the secrecy of a carnival mask.
The scent of the evening breeze
Comes to my mind like a mist
Which others' senses cannot grasp,
Because what I left behind,
Faraway, in another land,
Nothing else can make up or match;
And the splashing of the paddle wheel,
Pushing along the Delta Queen,
Keeps me safe and frozen in time,
Away from the hustle and bustle
Controlling everyone on board,
But me within my daydream.

Loneliness Within a Delta Queen Crowd

He was in his teens, trying to do away
With his social loneliness
And also with his spiritual emptiness
And his orphan-like feelings,
Trying to be with the crowd, how
To become one of them,
How to leave out what he is, become
An indifferent human
And take on the way they relate to nature and themselves.
Saint Louis and the huge Mississippi
Were right there before him,
With the hustle and bustle of the Midwest-summer time
And the smiles-shaping mouths, faces, eyes and hair.
Bodies of all kinds, sizes and shapes,
Masked in different ways:
Dresses, shoes, hats, pants bought at the same places.

He walked in the crowd, not with it,
Because he was different and no one
Could see that he was alone.
The Delta Queen had been waiting
Seasons and years, indifferent:
Laughter, the calliope's tunes, the sun
In the horizon going down
And the mad, muddy waters looked
Indifferent about everything,
Getting away from the Delta Queen and him, too.
Indifferent to his loneliness in a self-
Contained, lonely crowd,
Not concerned about his loneliness, just like the sun
Getting away from the river's current,
The Delta Queen and him.

Self-Search

And life has gone over its hills,
Across its rivers, into the dark
Of the mountains of their personal life;
Into the depth of the jungle of those around
Who believed that they are in the final count
To become aware that theirs is the best
And most valued, without being sure to be so,
Whether they knew it or not.

They were suppressed by those who have,
That which others don't have
For they missed it because they couldn't grasp it,
And that's what life could be about,
But when they acquired what they lacked,
They scanned those who did have
And said to themselves, "Now what?"

We have to search in our innermost,
To find whatever we should want:
To improve upon our "selves,"
And let others know that that which we need
Is not necessarily what they want or have,
But our very own thinking, feelings,
Lifestyle and self-image and that's exactly,
What you and I should really search for.

Happiness

Happiness did not leave you.
You just put it to sleep
Through anxiety, sorry moods,
Thinking that life is always smooth,
Or dealing with things unforeseen.
You need to wake up,
Stop looking around
To get it from others,
And blame your "amore."
Happiness is a valuable gift
That you stored down so deep
To find comfort in your "licore"
And forgot it was there.
If life passes you by
And no one to you comes near,
Remember to search not around
But turn yourself inside out
To see that happiness abounds.

Society's Changing Ways

It is happening this very moment everywhere,
While humanity is carrying out its
Addictive behavior guidelines,
Trying to implant positives to replace negative ones.
And this is happening right under
Your almost-know-it-all eyes,
Eyes that can see almost everywhere most of the time,
In the metropolis worldwide, including
Out-of-the-way places,
And wherever you are:
Humans coming and going or just standing by
But doing whatever assures them of their status,
Which makes them feel that they are
Whatever they need to be:
The worker working for wages on-the-job-training site
Or occupationally trained, applying
Acquired technical skills;
The professionally trained, applying what he/she knows,
To give hope and to improve one's self-image and love;
The gang member and those who are not
But should, at least be honorary members,
Whether they know it or not.

And all above humans do their own
Thing through politics, religion,
Education, science,
Worshipping their "Selves" through ignorance,
Kindness, unkindness, schooling and industrial training,
Giving of themselves or others, being eloquent
To impress friends, relatives,
Co-workers, electorates, social,
Educational, political, scientific,
Pseudo-artistic entrepreneurs
And pseudo-miracle performers.
It is a 24/7 hourly effort trying, doing, succeeding, failing
And trying again and again
For personal gain and purpose,
Which may be accomplished only if
Tolerance, humility, honesty,
Fairness and endurance are some of
The ingredients prescribed
To accomplish what one wants, if one really wants it
Without setting one's personal price.
Do not look around for anyone to
Accomplish what you need or want:
Society always rewards the positive side of your life.

The Cloud is Always Present

A protective cloud
With a silver lining,
A hidden message
Which you never see
If no one points it out.
It is hiding in your mind,
But ready to come out
And show
That you were not right
When you thought
The bad was always nearby.
It is the cloud within you,
Confined to your innermost,
Something that through life
You never thought you had,
And you could access
When everything looked bad,
And when life to you
Appeared utterly sad.

In Good Taste

Moths are not careful bugs
And to prove it he has a wool sweater
With a hole in front,
Not by choice, of course.
But this adventurous moth
Got in the house, went straight to his closet,
Landed on his sweater
And chop, chop, chop,
A big hole through the front,
Big enough to show the color
Of the shirt, which he may be wearing.
Now he has to buy a shirt,
The same color as his sweater,
To wear around farsighted folks
Or those who don't care
That the hole is there,
Or anyone who might look through
And not become despaired
By the disguise of the hole
Of the matching-style wear.

Getting a Haircut

A neighbor went to a barber,
A pretty lady of deep-blue eyes,
And she called herself a lady of style
Making the customer believe,
That she could make anyone look sharp.
His hair, actually, didn't look too bad,
And he wasn't concerned,
For he was already past thirty-nine.
And she said, "Hi, I am Barb. Tell me
Who you are."
And he answered, "My name is Art."

"Please sit in that chair but be careful
Not to hit your knee on the side-metal bar."
Lifting a strand of his see-through hair

With fingers of both hands:
"Do you want it shorter, the same,
Or, is it entirely up to me?"
"I trust your skill, do as you please.
Just don't turn your scissors into a mill."
And chop . . ., chop . . ., chop in front,
On top, sides, and behind.
And when he saw his hair in the mirror,
He jumped off the barber's chair,
Gave the self-professed stylist a tip
Along with a nice-courteous-thank-you-smile
For all through the shearing
She didn't show any experience or training
But she was extremely friendly,
And simply, trying very hard.

Rain Dance

Drops and droplets dancing on the roof,
On the driveway car tops,
Out in the street and the front yard, too.
From tapping to waltzing
And doing the blues,
From fast to slow, back and forth;
A celebration symphony
With the tree leaves,
At times listening,
At times performing
The dance of the rain:
Drops and droplets intoxicated
With nature's joy,
Dancing in the trees,
Skipping down their trunks,
Racing over the sidewalk,
Announcing to all
That the drought is gone
And the sunshine is welcome
To drink of nature's joyful flow.

Nature's Transitional Design

Not impulsed by wind, snow, rain or breeze,
Flutter between the branches the gilded leaves,
Lighted in the down journey by the sun beams,
Oscillating as they descend, almost at will.
They fall because their time has ended:
No sap to keep the green, no life to share.
Sap has been intended
To keep the tree from always being bare,
To display a passing beauty, as expected.
When the wind blows the leaves seem to jump off,
Aligned in the direction in which it goes
And they fly away in linear perfection,
Swaying up and down, without failing to adjust
To a perfect artistic conception.
And I know that leaves like human lives,
Will someday fall and decompose,
To feed the ground, to stage another passing show.

Joyful-Time Fusion

Just yesterday
He was climbing guava trees,
Eating their fruit and watching
The birds peck . . ., peck . . ., peck . . .,
Swallowing the seeds
To drop undisclosedly,
Somewhere in the jungle
A new generation of trees.
He was barely aware of the moment
But now sees the experience
As wonderfully nice.
He cannot see the relevance of time:
Now is yesterday, stored for tomorrow
In a life span.
There are no time barriers
In the universe
And tomorrow, yesterday, today,
Always happen,
At some point in time,
To be the same.

Alcohol-Created Monster

I remember my father, on the floor,
Across the front entrance door:
A French butcher knife flat on his chest,
Snoring like a monstrous beast
Defeated by countless alcoholic drinks,
Since before I was conceived,
Muttering under his breath
Unmentionable words to my mother,
And all of us seven kids in the household.
I remember tiptoeing and trembling with fear,
To the only way out to the sidewalk,
As quiet as a trapped mouse.
All moving in a single file,
Stepping over his stinking body:
One foot at a time,
And then looking back,
Hoping for the one behind to survive the escape:
One . . ., two . . ., three . . ., four . . .,
Five . . ., six . . ., seven . . .,
And my mother last to go over the dormant body,
Headed nowhere, in search of food and love.

A Never-Ending-Western Search

A fourth of a pie: the western plains
Converging with the sky,
Beyond the North Platte River
And across buffalo land.
I can hear it and see it
On my never-ending tape:
The roaring of the hooves,
While the moonlight pierces my skull
And steadies my nerves,
Right within my brain.
And inside my mind,
I see the fourth of a pie,
Comprising the light
Reflecting off the North Platte River,
But further than the western domain,
Over the Rocky Mountains:
Majestic guard surveying the plains,
And admiring the sky.
But the tape is fading
And I must wait
To continue searching
For the end of the fourth of the pie.

That's Where He Was Born

He was born on the mountain range;
Where the breeze caresses his neck and face,
And the imagination daily excites his brains,
Runs wild and frees his life from any pain;
Where the wind defeats the sunshine rays,
And the pasture, the trees and the grass
Are warehouses for fowl, four-legged creatures,
And sometimes adventurous boys and girls.
The river ignores nature's charm,
Nurtures turtles, fish and crabs,
And digs soil from the side of the hill
Along with precious nuggets of gold.
Where the mountain lion roars
And all the animals heed their king's voice;
The oceans simultaneously press
Against both sides of the land,
And volcanoes pierce the clouds
To look into the skies.

When the moon shines,
It makes the foliage resemble emerald blocks
And filters its beams through the green
To see the fish jump into the darkness
And turn into silvery lances.
The transparent waters in the upstream creek,
Even after midnight hours,
Sing to the grass and the trees.
The clinging vines descend from on high
Right above the aquatic surface
For a kiss from the misty air of the night;
The fish are the target of the moon beams
Which ride on the fish' nape
Up and down with the waves
As they sway like a merry-go-round.
Where life in the air, soil and water abounds,
The sky is blue all day long,
And showers come torrentially and quickly go;
But the evening darkness is dissipated by a starry host:
That's where he was born!

A New Bird House

Tweet, tweet, tweet,
Sing the baby birds
In their colorful new house,
Painted blue, white and green,
Way up in the air,
On a wooden platform
At the end of a metal pipe,
Under a branch of a locust tree,
Protected from the rain and the wind.
And they keep on chirping:
Tweet, tweet, tweet,
Thanking the builders
For their colorful home.
And half-way through the spring,
Open beaks one can see
Begging for food,
Not just from anyone
But from their mommy bird
That comes flying in
With big, fat worms in her beak,
To quiet down
The starving baby birds.

Real Founders

The sparks of the blacksmith's craft . . ., the anvil;
A leg of the mount firmly held in his hand,
Generating awareness that the blacksmith's prowess
Is his ultimate command!

It was not only the jet setters
Who forged our nation's pride,
Nor the religious leaders
Proclaiming religion in the cities
And the countryside
Who made our nation's
Mores and possessions abound.
It was also the farmers and ranchers,
The steel forgers and miners,
The trappers and the loggers
Who made the way to their adventures,
Worked like social indentures
To proclaim our human rights,
To find freedom to work the land,
To make this nation the hope,
The dream that other countries
Would like to have and make it materialize.
It is you and I, too.
And those left behind.

Nocturnal Rain Reflections

The tap . . ., tap . . ., tap . . ., on the roof
Announcing that it is time
To look out the window . . ., outside
To capture the brilliance on the pavement,
The brilliance in the lightness
Of the light reflections,
Gradually outlining the shape of the trees,
The flowers along the sides of the driveway
And everything else within one's vision field,
With the clock watching
And its ticktock superstitiously
Claiming one's life one second at a time,
In this beautiful, terrestrial land.
Not that it matters, whenever we part,
For life is just one more device
For all of us at this planet,
Temporarily to reside with nature's beauty
Which comes, of course, from our peace of mind.

Silent Sounds

The silence of the heart
And of the mind
Which makes the sounds,
On and off,
In images which tell the world
That it never was
From the future or the past.
And that is why
It never left
Any track behind.
It is the silence
Of the artistic mind,
Which funnels like a twister
Into the human sentimental blank,
Looking for peace and calm
But explodes . . ., in intertwined colors,
Tremulous symphonic vibrations,
Or soothing poetic lines.

Rhythmical Return

The murmur of the wind . . .
The crystal-clear tone of a liquefied serpent
Sliding along the mountain side,
To flee away from the sierra top:
Feelings diluted by the thought
Of golden rays riding the waves
On the continuous aquatic drain,
Disappearing through a nebulous night,
Until dawn brings them down again
To repeat the experience of another sun delight:
The vision of the adventure of a child
Of an innocent pastoral site
Surrounded by green covers at either side,
Which the human eye can never disregard
Along the serpentine fountain rout
Proceeding to a common nest,
Wherein it may or may not rest.
But it will certainly ascend vaporized,
To come back to wander
And later on to be transformed into rain.

The Process

One breath . . ., a converging point:
Two angular energy trails
Enclosing the winds,
The rain and the clouds,
Or the sunshine of daily life . . .,
Tears of existence
Intertwined with signs of being,
Prompting a becoming.
An eternity waiting for the cry:
Just air in the id
To create a self
And go through life,
May be not to engender
But to surrender
To time and the incline.
But the creation is an image
That lives forever
In the Creator's realm . . .,
A mystery to the human mind.

A Princess and a Saint

Almost simultaneously departed from earth
Who served the kingdom of heaven's heirs,
Declared so in biblical terms.
One prevented violent annihilation
For the sake of human ease;
The other, death and misery,
By feeding and comforting
The downhearted, always in need.
There were no gaps in-between:
One lived in majestic palaces,
The saint, in dwellings of peace
But the pain to both was the same.
Empathy has no physical barriers
And negative feelings come from distress.
It makes no difference
That one was a princess,
The other . . ., a humble saint.

Looking for Life's Dream

He was born to the clear-water streams
To share with others fish, fowl,
And the adventurous breeze caressing
Wild beasts, sunshine rays,
And smiling at trees,
But unaware of what, when,
Or how much to achieve:
Like he.
He is a very porous sponge now,
Ready to capture and sift through,
To reject whatever floats,
And dive for life's golden nuggets
Deep under the stream's current,
And like the breeze and he,
Everyone needs energy and faith
To be propelled by visionary dreams,
Until one comes to one's open space,
To be what one always dreamed:
One's self in one's immortal field.

The Cricket Within

A cricket creaking:
You can feel its legs angling up;
Its tiny wings ready to pluck the notes,
Ready to play a nightly melody.
It is not in the house, nor up in a tree,
On a safety limb.
Believe it or not, it is in you.
The you "self," which puts out feelers
For your cricket
To sneak in undetected,
To chirp when it gets in your cellar,
The cellar which your mind may unlock
To listen to your self's cricket
Playing one's emotional nightly song.
And you can hear it and feel it,
Perceive it all night long
But to touch it with your feelers
It is, of course, a no-no.

Another Storm

There is a storm again,
Humanly measurable by depth,
By humans with empty eyes,
Unable to perceive, without eyesight;
But the trees house it,
For it falls free
And sticks to the bark, leafless twigs,
Roofs and pavement everywhere.
Strange! Humans and storms
Have never learned to properly interact.

Compressed behavior dressed in white,
Behavior in white that never dies,
Never feels the cold, never feels
What life is really about;
But later on it shows up in green,
Crystallized or liquefied,
To feed the green and be on earth,
Everywhere in multiple colors,
To feed nature, to nurture humanity
In life's spring and summer time,
Until later on, when it reappears
Dressed again
In the usually, expected white.

Sunlight Ray of Hope

There is not even a song
From the muses tonight.
Away have they gone
Never to return,
Unless life again is right.
He knows not where is their abode
But he knows their love to him
Is always near.
Empty is the nest
Where bundles of joy
Used to remain, all alone,
Until life's anxieties
Started to come along.
And he knows that this emptiness
Will only take a sunlight ray,
To light up the space
With an explosion of love
That will give life again,
An inspirational golden glow.

The Drilling-Fan-Red-Rabbit Rose

A red-rose bud approaching
His insight vision field.
It floats slowly forward
As it turns into a power drill.
His "self" backs off
And upon doing so,
It turns to the flower stage
And opens up into a rose,
Full-fledged,
Before changing to a fan
Rotating in advance.
As he closes his mind
For protection from the asps.
It stops turning and changes fast
Into a rabbit, standing, looking out.
Then, opens up he his mind
To find his "self"
Floating in a cloud,
Away from his domain.

Euphoric White

There is an immaculate blanket
Spread over the streets, houses
Big and small and between the trees.
There is no breeze
Disrupting anyone's inner peace,
Which is here tonight but not so in May,
When winter has, as it may,
Receded to the past
And the spring-like rain,
Hurrying to awaken and pull out the leaves,
Has come down to us to ease off the pain
Of remembering the white,
Which in the not-remote past
Gave out a beautiful
And serene peace of mind.

So . . ., let me step outside
And gaze into the mystery of the night
Which may carry you and me
To dream of the passing
Euphoric white.

Inner-Peace-Winter Reflections

A cold Rocky Mountain morning,
Cold, of course, for some humans only.
A branch of a European-ash tree
Extends above the deck and on a leafless twig,
An-almost-symmetrical-brown ball of feathers,
A sparrow, stands away from its flock.
It takes turns picking and swallowing
Dried up berries from summers past,
And after each food treat, it scoops up
Powdery snow from its surroundings,
And its itsy-bitsy eyes shine unconcerned,
But happy, perhaps, about its early-morning meal.

On the sidewalk, a rabbit hops slowly,
Shifty eyes, twitchy ears and nose,
Watching for any green to show
Above the slanted-sidewalk snow,
While the snow storm persists
And a Canadian goose flies in the grayish-dark space,
Indifferent about life below, but scanning
For some feeding-field to land upon.

The sparrow, the rabbit and the Canadian goose
Are just reflecting their inner peace,
Which I really own.

Spring-Time Flowers

There will be flowers
After the rain:
Deep blue, light yellow,
Looking up to the sky
For the comfort and delight
Of those passing by.
Smiling-like faces,
Not from winter time
For the snow is cold
And spring-time flowers
Need to reflect
Their beautiful glow,
The sunshine rays
That come and go,
The light that makes them grow
White, blue or yellow gold,
To the contentment
Of those who need,
Or want to give love.

Invitation

The leaves
Of the locust tree,
Outside
My bedroom window,
Moved by the breeze,
Move with movements
Which tell me:
"Come up here
And join us to see
That children,
As well as insects and birds,
And other things
Up in this tree
Crave your company,
For you to enjoy, to see,
Things that you cannot perceive
Unless you are with us,
To feel the way we feel,
As part of this beautiful tree.

The Lonely Leaf

In the driveway,
Almost under the left front tire,
With light brown colors,
Separated from darker tones:
Crystal-white underside,
And white powder on top
From the night before,
Giving way to a two-tone design,
Lays away from its habitation source
An aspen leaf battered by the wind.
It descended with snow flakes
That fluttered down
With other leaves,
Swaying in the cold-blasting air
As frigid as the inconspicuous leaf
Protecting the mystery
Of its white underneath,
Intact, immaculate like an angel's face,
Insulated from its superficial brown
Ignored by every passerby
Who may never see the beauty
Which holds together
The fine-arts designs
In the gloomy side of life.

Communication Styles

Traveling by air, land or waterways,
One never knows how to prepare
And one can only use
Whatever for the occasion fits,
Not what those around may recommend.

How you think goes along
With whatever language style
You use to communicate:
Body language, gestures, empathy,
Voice volume and intonation,
To tell the message receiver(s)
What cultural environment
You came from.

And mannerisms which you may use
Through your self-image mouth;
How you perceive messages
From those around,
And how you reflect them back,
Will show others
What you really are like.

Cowboy at a Truck Stop

A huge stack of pancakes,
Butter and syrup covering the mound
Almost as big around as his cowboy hat,
And black coffee to wash them down.
Behind the scuffed boots, the sharp spurs;
A real leather-sheep-fleece jacket,
Eyes glued on his breakfast delight:
"Howdy, pardner." "Not a drugstore cowhand?"
"No, sir, cattle and horses are my life."
He grins, his eyes open up like bright stars,
His mouth stretches wide,
And his whole personality bubbles
Like flashing back a ride in the meadow,
Under the blue sky,
With the sunshine and the breeze behind,
Happily chasing his last round-up cow.

Selves Sameness

In and out like in a maze, two bobbins
Pointing the thread to the eye of the needle,
Disguising different changeable time frames,
Both seeking a value-goal-oriented place
Before the spool's content comes to an end,
And looking for the appropriate space
Where the selves' conformity may find a nest,
Unaware that spirit and matter from any site
May, without warning, dissipate.
One "self," unconcerned, may separate
To justify becoming, but disregarding
That the double, by going the distance
May qualify to try
For whatever the trial may be,
But the needle keeps going through
The social fabric tenaciously and fast
Looking for the right self-accepting style,
Always pointing the way to the thread:
The need for pursuing becoming
In any country, society or race,
Before the spool's content comes to an end,
Not realizing that for any entity, anywhere,
Any kind of becoming requires a process
Which is always, for any "self," the same.

Tropical Nocturnal Art Sketch

The emerald-green cover of the jungle,
The platinum spray in the air
Illumined by the light of the lunar rays,
The singing of the fountain
Skipping around the hillside
At a night festival
With the harmony of a waterfall;
The pounding of my heart,
In a thatch-roofed loft
Watching a mountain-lion pride
Sharpening their claws on a tree trunk
And taking turns roaring all night long;
The monkeys howling in the tree top,
While the jungle tries to repose
From its daily tropical-heat dose,
Mesmerized by so much wonder,
And I, inspired by the collective art
Which my spiritual eyes
Capture through the dark,
Feel like an insignificant element
From the Majestic Painter's brush.

Napping in the Sunshine

Catching a few rays on a limb,
Not bigger around than a thumb,
In a huge tree by the house deck,
There is a baby squirrel
Unjittery, calm, dozing off:
It's tail not a twirling baseball bat,
Its head not a swivel screw,
The round tiny twig its mat,
The sun and nature claims as its own.
Not a twinkle in its eyes,
Not a chirp from its mouth,
Caring not what one might think or say,
Now sleeps sound
The cute rodent,
In the early morning sunshine.

Spring Cattle-Branding Time

The cool breeze of the mountain valley
Refreshing the humid vegetation
Under the tall trees at the mountain/pasture threshold.
The birds announcing to dawn
That it is time to depart once more
And under the trees, the top-dog cowboy,
From under a dusty blanket, pokes his face out
To yell an order to his cowhands,
To get up to eat the flapjacks
And crispy fried bacon,
That the chuck-wagon cook had been frying
For many hours before chow time.
Bright flames light the way
For dawn to bring in the day
And the cook fills the mugs
From a pitcher sitting over the triangular space,
Enclosed by three flat-top rocks,
Surrounded by blue and yellow dancing flames
Hanging from a heavy column of smoke,
Curling up amidst the ash flakes
Peppering the bacon, the fried eggs,
And sticking to the syrup on the pancakes.
The clanking of dishes and spoons, forks and knives,
And then . . .: "Get the irons ready."
"Hold that dogie down." And the shhhhhhhhhhh,
With a puff of smoke just before the fur-hide stink,
Makes clear letterforms on each side
Within a triangular figure: SLM (suffering, life, money).
And then . . ., "Get the next one down!"
This is spring cattle-branding time.

The Rain Outside

The rain tonight I know is falling outside
But somehow, a phonic message it sends to my heart
And turns it into pictures that I cannot describe
Because they are the frame of my artistic mind:
One could be a camp-ground pond
Crowded by Rocky Mountain trout
Or the tropical-rain-forest umbrella
Dripping off for miles and miles
Into an aquatic highway,
Dashing away to the ocean bluish mat.
Another could be the tears in my eyes
That nor tonight or ever anyone could understand.
And the rain outside does not realize,
How much it is affecting,
The way I really am.

You: My True Love!

You were my reason,
Years and years ago
To fly from the south,
To fly north
In search of love.
You were my reason
To fly to the west,
To love you more and more;
You were in my destiny,
Well knows it The Lord.
In His eternal planning,
He planned it to be so.

You are the reason
For my existence,
Whether you know it or not,
And I have flown
From the south
Along with the wind,
The rain, sunshine and snow,
Not to achieve prestige
And honors,
But to let you know,
That you are my true love.

Cheyenne's Mystery Land

On the plains swept by ferocious winds:
Cowboy boots, hats and belts,
Embellished by—as expected—rattle-snake skin,
Surviving the snow
And the sunrays scorching heat,
Along with jackets, vests and cow-hide chaps
Saved for cattle roundups
Or while riding fence;
Then appears the merchant world
And the military,
Where you watch side by side,
The slim and not so slim:
Military personnel husbands and wives,
And left-over pioneers from past,
Historical Cheyenne Indian days:
Pioneer noses, eyes, ears, foreheads
Surrounded by platinum-white
Wind-tossed-coarse-grained hair,
Eating at fast-food places.
The Indian trading post
Has long being gone to museums
And out of the way places
But the memory of a glorious civilization
Lingers on in the epic
Of Wyoming's Cheyenne's Days,
Which carries you and me
Back to the foundation
Of the American Indian land
And the Cheyenne Indian Braves.

Quiet Wisdom

Flashes of quietness zigzagging,
Plucking out mysteries of soundness:
Concepts not perceived,
Nor seen by eyeless minds . . .
Floating in space,
Never by the human mind assessed.
There is crying:
Ongoing and from yesteryear,
There is laughter in the distance,
There is whispering and yelling
And vague human thoughts
Of all kinds, undistinguishable,
Enmeshed and trapped in the webs
Of things that are, that were
Never to arrive, never to depart,
Just trapped in the quietness
Within the human mind:
Closeness that keeps one safe
In the vacuum of a dormant
Human vein.

Metaphor

The aspens are gathered tonight
In circular formation:
Under a platinum disc
Hidden in the dark clouds,
Which are unable to hide
The brilliance around them.

They stand
Like gossiping announcers,
And have no choice
But to spread the leaves out
To let the lunar rays proceed
Through my window panes
To bring a message to captive eyes,
Not reflecting but absorbing
The news of joy in the mind,
Which prints the picture
Of poetic prose, of symphonic music,
And of frescoes
To remain forever alluring,
Through the inspiration
Of the melody of beauty,
Of the poem of joy, the poem
That humanity will always
Dearly love.

Visual Creations

A bright-blue cascade of flowers!
One wonders where they go,
Where they are coming from!
They may come from a trap in the brain,
Which has accidentally opened up
And spilled into one's eyes,
For one to introspect about.
With one's eyes closed in the dark,
One can see that the cascade
Does not reach the ground,
But from a mountain-top spillway
It floats away in the passive air,
In infinite number of particles.
The blue-microscopic flowers
Move away gracefully,
Casually floating . . ., disintegrating . . .,
Disappearing from the vision screen
And have faded out
Before closing one's eyes
For the expected nocturnal journey,
Of one's rest-craving temporal life.

Spiritual Rest in a Snow Storm

A prelude . . .? An overture . . .?
To the undisclosed symphony
Of the day's pre-determined
But unconsigned musical tones
Dripping down
From the Rocky Mountain sky.
I am sitting inside, by the deck door,
Like attendants at any symphony performance,
Ceremoniously waiting for the Master
To strike down the magical baton
And shatter the barriers
Of mysterious notes
Never by anyone heard before.

Straight down,
Between and among the trees,
Houses, fences, traffic, fields,
Cities, countryside, lakes and everywhere,
My soul watches the continuous
But evenly interrupted silvery threads
Softly rest at the majestically, pre-assigned
Symphonic, synchronized
Rhythmical spaces,
To make this a day of spiritual rest
In the symphony
Of this white-Christmas-like snowfall,
Filling our lives
With beauty and peace
In our souls.

Quaking Aspen Leaves

Like trembling ballerinas
Adorning the trees,
Flutter the green leaves
Of the quaking aspens
Obeying the passing winds
Of the Rocky Mountain Spring.
Green leaves only for the Spring.
The autumn cold changes them
To gold yellow
As sweet as the sugar cane.
Is it not vain
That the human mind
Does not care to understand,
That it is not the yellow
That makes the change,
But the sweetness
Behind the goldenness
That is passing by
And turns the leaves
Into a self-effacing brown,
With the traveling of fall
And winter time!

Call of the Jungle

One can hear the echo
From the tropical paradise,
Where the soil is solid black,
The trees compete
To look up to the sky
And their roots peek through,
To catch some fresh air
Above the ground.
When it rains,
The rivers run over the banks
And the soil is so soft,
That armadillos do not have to dig
In the ground to find shelter;
The benevolent earth opens up
For the armored creatures
To crawl in to rest, or at night.
One can hear the call of the jungle,
Calling you and me
To taste of the wild fruit
Falling underneath the trees,
All around you and me:
In the rainforest jungle,
With nature and the wild beasts.

Honey-Bee Smarts

Honey bees are smarter
Than one may think.
When there is a blizzard
They stay in the hive
And share their own
Individual warmth
With all the workers inside.
They see the rain and snow,
Close tight their eyes
And fill their brains
With mental pictures
Of beautiful aroma flowers
On green meadows and valleys,
Where they can fly searching
For vetch, alfalfa, mustard,
And many more blooming plants,
But only after scouting
Parks, private gardens
And even alleys,
To avoid wasting resources
Where they can gather pollen
To make wax
And fill the frames
In their honey-storage boxes
With six-sided-wax cells,
To store the honey,
To feed their colony
Past the time
When honey-making season is over.

Finding One's Dream

He was born
Around the clear-water streams
To share with others, fowl, fish,
And the adventurous breeze
Caressing wild beasts,
Sunshine rays,
And smiling at trees,
But unaware of what, when,
Or how much to achieve, like he.
For he is a sponge,
Ready to capture and sift through,
To repel whatever floats,
And dive for gold nuggets
Down at the bottom,
Under the current;
And like the breeze,
Everyone needs energy and faith
To be propelled by visionary dreams,
Until one comes to one's open space,
To be what one always dreamed:
One's self in one's immortal field.

Farewell in the Sugar-Cane Field

She led him gently by his hand
Into the luscious sugar-cane field,
Oscillating as the breeze of the tropical land,
Between the feet and the ground, a fluffy shield.

The stars and the moon platinum light,
Almost as bright as her glowing eyes:
"Let us stop here for it is almost midnight."
And she tenderly looked into his eyes.

Finally, a sweet-farewell kiss of love,
Oblivious to the starry sky above.

Spring-Time Aroma

A fragrance of spring-time arrival
From a blooming-golden-locust tree,
Outside the bedroom window sill
And it is almost midnight,
A few minutes before
The 12:00 o'clock mark.

The breeze brings in the sweet aroma
Which not everyone may enjoy,
For not everybody is endowed to perceive
The nocturnal-time inspiration
Through the force intensity of the essence,
Which keeps some from investing
The effort required to photograph with words
What is needed to go on living one's life.
There is also a full-moon's light,
Pushing the breeze and cool air
Over one's body, toes to hair;
And the moon's brightness spreads out
Embracing also all the Rocky Mountain terrain.

At the Carwash

It is coming at you!
Pounding on the roof,
Flapping around,
Rubbery-devil red,
Maybe gray, the color of death;
Boiling or ice-cold water,
Really scary, anyway.

Your wife laughs
When you say to her,
"Hopefully I'll see you soon,
And if things go well,
In just a few."
She insists that you put it through,
Just to prove that you are not
As brave as you think you are,
And maybe, hoping
That you won't be found
Stiff dead
From a heart attack,
In the neighborhood carwash.

Unreality

Floating in the air,
Through non-existing eyes,
One sees sadness waves
Which do not exist.
One can perceive a mist
In yonder light
Which seems to be in the dark . . .,
But so far apart
From one's mind
That distance cannot reconcile
Mind and light,
Dark and sight
In anyone's existence:
Sensations no one can grasp,
Turning into feelings of heaviness
In one's soul,
Mixing process and content
Within one's heart.

Labor's Rewards

You spread feelings around you
Like the farmer spreads seeds
On the field seedbeds all day long, irrigates
And his seeds sprout and grow.
The farmer plows while his mind captures
The rows and rows of a bountiful crop,
As the plow breaks the soil,
Or the discs go around
Cutting dirt lumps to prepare the field
And make the furrows
Where the newly sprouted plants
May grow and thrive.

You wake up in the morning,
Look around and smile,
Announcing to your surroundings
That you are ready to face it all
And that is your daily crow!
And those around you, in turn,
Love the way you show your feelings
Then and all day long: the way you smile,
The way you look at others
And your tone of voice,
Your way of saying with your body language,
"I love you so and hope that today,
I may be to you, a happy new song,
To sing it at work, wherever you are,
All day long."

Nature's Peaceful Love

Let the trees sing spring songs . . .,
And let the wind whisper words of love,
Words of love to the branches
Where the birds perch and chirp
As they go to sleep until dawn,
When the light starts to ride
Out of the darkness of the night just past
And let dawn be nature's moat: the right road
To the castle of your personal love,
And let life's love turn into restful peace,
Peace that may influence you to cherish love,
Love for those who may need you,
Peace that you may see
Over the calm waters
Of a lake or a tranquil sea,
That you may see in the horizon,
Between the trees
Unable to hold back the sunshine light
From shining on your life's night,
Peace that you may always feel,
Wherever you may be.

Floating Down the River

Floating down the river,
No place to go,
Up and down with the waves,
Left and right
And around with the wind,
In the company of care-free birds
That fly, dive or swim
In search of something to eat.
Your back caressed
By the cool feeling underneath,
Your front caressed
By the solar beams,
Your mind void of concerns,
Your heart, full of joy.

The Squirrel in the Tallest Tree

Up in the biggest-back-yard tree,
Lives a squirrel which is very friendly,
And likes people like you and me.
Late in the afternoon
He climbs way up in the tallest branch,
And sits, very relaxed, in the highest bough
To enjoy the sunset,
And sometimes to watch a rainbow glow;
Once in a while he invites all his friends,
From all the neighborhood trees
To chatter, to run around or just to be with.
He likes to hang upside down
With nuts, dry crab apples or seeds
In his mouth and he loves doing that
Because it makes him feel like a circus clown.
When the sun rises,
He runs up and down the branches,
Looking for food to store for winter time,
When everything is under snow,
And squirrels cannot find food anymore.

He hides whatever he finds
In his favorite flower box
And when it is time to eat,
He forgets where he hid it all;
Then, he stands on the edge of any box
And thinks . . ., thinks . . ., thinks . . .
But cannot remember
Where he hid the food at all
And goes back to the tree
To play some more;
Then, before sunset and bed time,
He tries once more to find the stash
Which he hid before—after eating
All day long—without having any luck,
But goes to bed and dreams of eating
Every nut he hid the day before
In his favorite flower box.

Peace Roses

Peace roses guarded by moonlight,
Under a black-walnut tree
Almost on the sidewalk,
At the edge of an evergreen hedge
Bordering the driveway;
Its roots spreading out
To explore under the surface of the street;
A yellow-pale hue absorbed in the morning
From fulminating sunbeams,
And the petals freshly cleansed
By the dew, dawn after dawn,
Frail but protected
By the walnut-tree shade,
And saturated with ethereal fragrance:
Euphoria-causing feelings
Day after day, night after night,
From early spring to late summer time.

The moon rays filter through the window glass
As we awake to the heat of the night
Announcing that we are coming
To another life's day's light
And to be silent and rejoice
In the sweet disruption of the peace roses,
Inviting through the breeze
To partake of the beautiful sensation:
The aromatic peace that anoints the soul,
And gets it ready to commune once more,
To display the purity through the petals,
For nature and passing admirers to enjoy.

Peaceful Love

Sweet, peaceful love
Is like the skin's tender touch
Of an Indian-summer rain
Which makes life glow with joy.

The Irish Whistle Notes

The Irish-Whistle-Musical Notes
Lose their names
And become a melody
As they come out of their
Musically assigned places
But they do not know
Whether they are flat or sharp;
And those tunes have to have freedom
To sound well at all,
And they really come out
Not from the Irish whistle,
But through the whistle pipe
They come out
From down deep
In the Irish soul,
The soul of the Celts,
Which one may capture
When playing the Irish whistle
To enhance one's joy,
To sooth one's sadness,
To fill with love one's soul.

A Dreamer's Two-Dream Fantasy

He dreamed of a verdant-mountain crest,
Where things would be what others always want:
A simple life and nothing else but rest
And pleasant sounds to cause untold enchant
In search of mental peace for mountain quest
And crystal water running down the slant.
The man, of course, enjoyed the dream a lot,
Awoke and wished to dream another plot:
The breeze ahead announcing possible risk,
A strong wind combing roofs along the way.
While looking out the jet, the speed seemed brisk.
How fun it was, of course, no one could say;
Around his house, his folks confused, dismayed.
Believe you me! He was prepared to fly.
He knew he could. He flew and was no lie.

Childhood Reality

Rushing through the pasture,
Four feet tall or so,
On foot or upon a horse,
His mind was out of control.
And he thought of himself
As being nature's lord:
The wind always behind.
Sometimes he could not realize
How euphoric he was
And he really believed
That he could fly and fly and fly . . .,
And vanish into the sky.
He could also go to the river
To bathe the neighbor's mare
And he would ride his friend
To the swimming hole
And not have to depend
On anything or anyone else at all.
He would imagine his steed
Could not only swim across
But also gallop on
To the mountain tops, over the range,
Across the valleys without a pause,
Ride over the horizon
Into the land of nevermore.

That is really what he thought;
And he never shared his visions
With any relative or friend.
Between the teacher and him,
Whenever he'd go to school
Something wonderful he would hear and see:
The pasture and the wind, the river, the valleys,
The mountain range, and going over the horizon,
The neighbor's mare and himself.

Tippy at the Dog Show

Tippy is funny,
Tippy is tiny
And goes to the fair
To show the judges
How clever she is
And to make people think
That she knows how to behave.
Katie her trainer,
Thinks that Tippy is cute
And gives her orders to obey,
And when that happens,
Tippy wonders,
Whether to run, to stay,
Or to prance
On her front or hind legs.

Tippy is beginning to find out
That the audience likes it
When she obeys
But the judges
Know not how to score
The way, sometimes,
Tippy behaves.
However, they think
That she is cute
And Katie is doing her best,
And that is why
They both got a blue ribbon
For taking first place
At the county fair.

Self-Protection

You arrive to the stream of life to face
The constant clang . . ., clang . . ., clang . . .,
To be part of the fountain of life
And you do it
In a loud anxious cry.
You, the new arrival,
Get used to the process of life,
Sometimes rejected, sometimes not,
With question marks
In-between both above.
But you need to ingrain in the "self,"
That life is good,
And the clang . . ., clang . . ., clang . . .,
In life's train cannot affect you,
If you keep in mind
That if others' behavior
Is not caused by your own,
You are not responsible for behavior
Which you did not cause,
And life's train's clang . . ., clang . . ., clang . . .,
Can go on and on,
Without affecting your personal life at all.

The Breeze, the Wind and the Willows

The wind and the willows
Seldom match skills:
One is swift,
The willows sway at ease.

The breeze is different:
Smiling as it arrives
To greet the willow trees,
Like a pleasant passerby.

Both, the breeze and the wind,
Are just like people,
Showing what they are.
Through usual behavior,
They show us
What life is about.

You are the breeze;
He, perhaps, the wind,
And the willows,
Those around us.

A Harpist's Dream

A harp player dreamed
That she was playing her harp,
And all the strings
Were of infinite length.
The melody was continuous
For each of them
And the tunes were
Tears of joy absorbed
By the night's dew
Turning into moon and sun rays,
Streams and rivers,
Waves of the sea
And the clashing from treetops,
Frightening those without faith,
But enhancing
The intensity of love everywhere.
The strings were melodious,
And the harmony, of course,
Keeping company with those
Who detect distress
Where there is none,
But the music went on and on,
Telling you, telling us that we all belong,
But not apart from the celestial
Strings-filled home, where harp music
Is just a show of love.

New Year's Resolutions

Repetition is the way of life,
And again comes
The end of the year's time:
Days, hours, minutes, seconds
And warnings, always about
Approaching the end of the line,
Which is alright,
And no one needs to feel sad
Because the end is coming,
Not as an expected surprise.

And it is not either
That time or life
Is going to stop at midnight,
Where a future ending
And a present time,
Necessarily need to overlap
About any new changes to survive;
And then, decisions may be made
About resolutions and promises,
As a personal plan
Not to keep for others but for yourself,
To improve the quality
Of your personal life
And to benefit relationships,
Distant and nearby, wherever you are.

Your Life's Seasons

It may be one of your life's winters;
If so, it is here
But you have survived so many
That you cannot remember
Where your life's winters have gone
With your emotional-weather snow.
Spring times were also here
And you enjoyed the blue skies,
The trees, the grass, the weeds and wild flowers,
Along with the rain and the sunshine,
And the Rocky-Mountain-style-spring times,
Will forever cling to your mind.
Summers have come and gone:
Outings and picnics with family and friends
Were the weekly trends,
To enjoy the sunshine again and again;
Full-moon nights through your windows
Came and went
But left an imprint in your brain.
Your life's-moon's light shone
Wherever you went;
Now your life's fall is nearing
And it is time to remember that life is kind,
And your life's autumn gracious,
Unforgettable and bright,
And you did your part very well,
Which is right.
It is time for your life's fall to arrive.
You did fine with what you had.

Called To Go Home

When the seconds, minutes, hours and days
Leave your house
And they slowly, one by one bid you bye,
The breath departs to vanish beyond the sky,
And there is no awareness
About life on earth anymore
For the soul has departed
Without telling the body that it is happening so.

When all the memories sift slowly
Like the sands in the funnel of a desert storm
And the wind incessantly blows,
The sand never returns to where it came from,
Then we know that those memories
Spread evenly in the minds of those
Who always loved Carol so,
And those who surrounded her
In the days before the storm,
Were not aware that the Majestic,
Forever-Loving Lord of all,
Was calling mom to go home.

A. Albert Aguero, Husband
January 13, 2014

Appendix

Sometimes we are affected by experiences in the present and from the past, which may have a tendency to turn into emotional problems. If ignored, these problems may hide down deep into our almost-unreachable innermost. We feel a spiritual loss expressed by accompanying feelings of loneliness, even when surrounded by friends and other loved ones. We question the purpose of our existence and sense a lack of meaning about our relationship with the universe. We actually get feelings of existential loneliness.

The author of the poem below, supplements above ideas when he says: "And yet, when we stop hurrying and worrying about the mundane things of life, there is a silence. But it is not the silence of emptiness, it is a silence filled with an intangible mystery," like in the following poetic stanzas of "Grey Leaves:"

Leaves of grey . . . may be a trick of the light.
Somewhere inside is an urgency,
Somewhere I cannot touch,
And I know I need, but I know not what
And I watch the leaves of grey
Through the window.
The trees are silent . . . but not really.
They stand thinking thoughts which take eons;
Thoughts they were thinking
When my ancestors stood here.
Their thoughts are peaceful.
They don't feel my need.

The sky is grey and silent,
Like the leaves of the trees,
And my soul aches, for I know not what . . .
For the peace in the boughs,
And leaves of grey trees,
For the time to understand
That my life is like the grey leaves:
A trick of the light.

Clifford S. Aguero

And he goes on to explain that ". . . the poem is about the transient and miraculous nature of life. Man hurries through life like so many creatures on this world, busy with the cares of home and providing the things necessary for life. Many of us rarely stop to ask questions that should really matter to us: Who am I? How did I get here? Why I am here? What is the nature of our world? . . ." And then, the poet goes on to clarify the meaning by making the following statement:

"The short explanation for this poem is that it speaks of the longing we feel inside to know the answers to the really big questions in life. Deep down inside is the silence and the knowledge few of us are able to unlock. We sense that something much greater is in there, but we cannot touch it, it is transient, like the shadows of leaves on the wall; when you reach out to touch them, they only move away from your touch. Life is beautiful and mysterious and our lot in life is to participate in the only way we know how, and that is mostly to be an observer."

From pre-birth to the end of the road, especially during childhood, we discovered and explored self-trails on carpets of beautiful green meadows inlaid with bright-multicolored-wild flowers. Those trails crossed over peaceful streams protected on both sides by tall grass with clusters where small fishes and aquatic insects hid as we approached and jumped over the stream, in some places with trees lining the banks of a wider-stream stretch, and day time or after dark, with sun or moonlight rays filtering through the emerald-green foliage, to light the way for the schools of fishes gliding peacefully on the way to nowhere.

Memories of above images can be re-created when in need of encouragement and hope, to go on living and remembering that life was good and full of love and can be so, again. And poetry is the means by which we can bring back our childhood memories and feelings and improve personal life quality. Dreams, fantasies, feelings and realities can be stored in poetic lines for present enjoyment and posterity reminiscence as seen in the masterly expressiveness of the following poem:

The Heart Knows

Home is where the heart is,
So far and yet so near;
The only place upon the earth,
So precious and so dear.

The honeysuckle on the fence,
That sweetly fills the air,
The paths so worn by children's feet,
The front-porch-rocking chair,

The green grass of summer,
The sassy mockingbirds,
Happy childish laughter,
Ringing through the woods,

The woodland path, the sycamore
Beside the little stream,
Where flowers bend to see their face
And silver fishes gleam,

The brilliant glow of sunset,
The fireflies in the dark;
Those things are like a picture,
Stamped forever in your heart.

No matter where you wander;
No matter what you seek;
Forever in your heart,
There skip these childish feet.

Carol Chalk Aguero